This is my doggo diary

Every page in this diary celebrates the special moments, big and small, that make my fur baby's life so extraordinary. It's where I write whenever something memorable happens - whether it's a silly joke, a milestone, or just a moment that fills my heart with love and joy. This diary is more than a collection of memories; it's a way to preserve my unique bond with my doggo. It helps me capture the laughter, the adventures, and even the quiet moments of comfort that define our time together.

Not only is this diary a keepsake I'll treasure forever, but it's also a practical record. It holds essential details like my dog's medical history, allergies, and favourite things, all in one place. Whether I'm looking back on cherished memories or needing to reference key information, this diary is always here for me. With each entry, I create a lasting memory of a life full of love, loyalty, and joy - a reflection of everything that makes my doggo special.

PET DETAILS

Your doggo's story starts here.

PET NAME:

DATE OF BIRTH:

BREED:

SEX:

COLOUR:

MICROCHIP:

SPECIAL MARKING:

PET PARENT DETAILS

NAME:

PHONE:

EMAIL:

ADDRESS:

MY DOGGO'S LIKES & DISLIKES

Because every doggo has favorites and fussies.

FAVOURITE FOODS:

FOODS MY DOGGO DOESN'T LIKE:

MY DOGGO'S LIKES & DISLIKES

Because every doggo has favorites and fussies.

FAVOURITE FOODS:

FOODS MY DOGGO DOESN'T LIKE:

MY DOGGO'S LIKES & DISLIKES

Because every doggo has favorites and fussies.

FAVOURITE ACTIVITIES:

DISLIKED ACTIVITIES:

MY DOGGO'S LIKES & DISLIKES

Because every doggo has favorites and fussies.

FAVOURITE ACTIVITIES:

DISLIKED ACTIVITIES:

CARE INSTRUCTIONS & ALERTS

Important notes for your doggo's comfort and safety.

ALLERGIES, SPECIAL NEEDS & ROUTINE:

CARE INSTRUCTIONS & ALERTS

Important notes for your doggo's comfort and safety.

ALLERGIES, SPECIAL NEEDS & ROUTINE:

VACCINATION

A healthy doggo is a happy doggo.

DATE	VACCINE	DUE DATE	VET

VACCINATION

A healthy doggo is a happy doggo.

DATE	VACCINE	DUE DATE	VET

VACCINATION

A healthy doggo is a happy doggo.

DATE	VACCINE	DUE DATE	VET

VACCINATION

A healthy doggo is a happy doggo.

DATE	VACCINE	DUE DATE	VET

VACCINATION

A healthy doggo is a happy doggo.

DATE	VACCINE	DUE DATE	VET

VACCINATION

A healthy doggo is a happy doggo.

DATE	VACCINE	DUE DATE	VET

VACCINATION

A healthy doggo is a happy doggo.

DATE	VACCINE	DUE DATE	VET

VACCINATION

A healthy doggo is a happy doggo.

DATE	VACCINE	DUE DATE	VET

VACCINATION

A healthy doggo is a happy doggo.

DATE	VACCINE	DUE DATE	VET

VACCINATION

A healthy doggo is a happy doggo.

DATE	VACCINE	DUE DATE	VET

DEWORMING

Keeping Tummies Healthy and Worm-Free.

DATE	AGE	WEIGHT	COMMENTS

DEWORMING

Keeping Tummies Healthy and Worm-Free.

DATE	AGE	WEIGHT	COMMENTS

DEWORMING

Keeping Tummies Healthy and Worm-Free.

DATE	AGE	WEIGHT	COMMENTS

DEWORMING

Keeping Tummies Healthy and Worm-Free.

DATE	AGE	WEIGHT	COMMENTS

DEWORMING

Keeping Tummies Healthy and Worm-Free.

DATE	AGE	WEIGHT	COMMENTS

DEWORMING

Keeping Tummies Healthy and Worm-Free.

DATE	AGE	WEIGHT	COMMENTS

DEWORMING

Keeping Tummies Healthy and Worm-Free.

DATE	AGE	WEIGHT	COMMENTS

DEWORMING

Keeping Tummies Healthy and Worm-Free.

DATE	AGE	WEIGHT	COMMENTS

DEWORMING

Keeping Tummies Healthy and Worm-Free.

DATE	AGE	WEIGHT	COMMENTS

DEWORMING

Keeping Tummies Healthy and Worm-Free.

DATE	AGE	WEIGHT	COMMENTS

LIFE'S HIGHLIGHTS

The journey is made of all kinds of memories.

LIFE'S HIGHLIGHTS

The journey is made of all kinds of memories.

LIFE'S HIGHLIGHTS

The journey is made of all kinds of memories.

LIFE'S HIGHLIGHTS

The journey is made of all kinds of memories.

This diary holds a heart

The Doggo Diary is more than just a journal - it's a heartfelt way to honour the cherished bond between a dog and its human. Thoughtfully designed by Dr. Gaurav Gulati, this diary was created to capture unforgettable moments, milestones, and memories, celebrating the joy and unconditional love dogs bring into our lives.

At Proficient Knowledge Group, we believe a dog is more than a pet; they're family. This diary helps preserve those special connections and memories that last a lifetime.

If you've found this diary, please understand its sentimental value. Contact the owner if their details are mentioned inside, or reach out to the Doggo Diary team through Dogopo.com to help reunite it with its rightful owner.

Let's treasure this extraordinary bond forever.

9 789334 428933